MARY AND HER MIRACLE

The Christmas Story Retold

☙☙☙

Mary and Her Miracle

The Christmas Story Retold

Barbara Cawthorne Crafton

MOREHOUSE PUBLISHING

An imprint of Church Publishing Incorporated

NEW YORK – HARRISBURG

Unless otherwise noted, the Scripture quotations contained herein are from the New Revised Standard Version Bible, copyright © 1989 by the Division of Christian Education of the National Council of Churches of Christ in the U.S.A. Used by permission. All rights reserved.

Morehouse Publishing, 4775 Linglestown Road, Harrisburg, PA 17105
Morehouse Publishing, 445 Fifth Avenue, New York, NY 10016
Morehouse Publishing is an imprint of Church Publishing Incorporated.

Cover and interior art by Dianne K. Robbins
Cover design by Brenda Klinger

Library of Congress Cataloging-in-Publication Data

Crafton, Barbara Cawthorne.
  Mary and her miracle : the Christmas story retold / Barbara Cawthorne Crafton.
     p. cm.
  ISBN-13: 978-0-8192-2148-3 (hardcover) 1. Jesus Christ—Nativity. I. Title.
  BT315.3.C73 2007
  232.92—dc22

                            2007026547

Printed in the United States of America

07 08 09 10 11 12   10 9 8 7 6 5 4 3 2 1

To the people of
the Church of the Resurrection
in Hopewell Junction, New York,
where Mary is honored and
her Son is worshipped
with great beauty and great love.
They have welcomed me
on many happy visits
and are always in my heart.

—Barbara Cawthorne Crafton,
The Geranium Farm, 2007

❧

Contents

Annunciation

MARY WAS SITTING, ALONE, in the garden behind her house. She was thinking. She had been spending a lot of time alone lately, thinking. Something important was about to happen to her.

She was going to be married. Her parents had just told her. She had never met Joseph, the man who was going to be her husband. Where Mary lived, girls didn't speak to men who were not their fathers or brothers. Never. It was not allowed. And when it was time for a girl to get married—when she was thirteen or fourteen—her parents decided who she would marry.

She was thinking about what it would be like. She would have to leave her mother and father and her brothers and their wives and all her nieces and nephews and cousins. She wouldn't be able to live in her own house any more. She hoped Joseph had a sister, or a girl cousin, and that his mother was nice. Mary's mother was her best friend. She looked up into the tamarind tree and her eyes filled with tears. She used to climb that tree when she was little. She had just climbed it a few weeks ago, and her mother had caught a glimpse of

9

her out the window. "Come down from there this minute, miss!" she scolded. Mary was too old to climb trees now. It was time to act like a lady, now that she was grown up enough to be married.

"Couldn't we wait a while?" Mary had asked her mother. "A couple of years, maybe? And then I could get married?"

Anna had reached for her daughter and held her close, stroking Mary's lovely black hair. Her eyes were brown like Mary's, and they looked now into the space just above Mary's head, at nothing in particular. She was thinking, too. Remembering. Anna had been thirteen when she married Mary's father. She hadn't wanted to leave home, either.

"Now, now, we'll visit back and forth. And then I'll come and help you with all your babies. You'll have—oh, I don't know—twenty-seven babies, maybe?" Anna was teasing.

Mary smiled a little. "Thirty-seven."

"You'll be too busy to miss Mama."

"No, I won't." Mary's lip trembled and her eyes filled with tears again. She pressed her face against her mother's chest and breathed in deeply through her nose. She loved the way her mother smelled. She didn't want to go and live with Joseph or anybody else. She wanted to stay home.

"It's because of the census, you know," Anna said. "Joseph has to go to Bethlehem and give an accounting of his family, and you're going to be part of his family. So he has to take you, too."

"The census is stupid. Counting people is stupid. What good is counting people?"

"Well, I guess the Romans like to count things," Anna said, giving Mary an extra hug and standing up. "Now, I'm going to go back inside and start supper. Are you going to help me or shall I make fifteen loaves of bread by myself?"

"I'll be there in just a minute." The sun was nearer to the horizon now, and it slanted through the leaves of the tamarind tree, making pools of golden light on the stone floor. The tamarinds hung from the branches all over the tree, plump and tempting. Late afternoon was a beautiful time.

You don't have to get married, you know, a voice said.

Mary looked around. Nobody was there.

Who's there?

I'm up here. The voice was coming from the tree. Mary looked up. Something glowing was perched in the spot where Mary usually sat when she climbed the tamarind.

Who are you?

My name is Gabriel.

I'm Mary.

I know.

How do you know about me? And that I'm getting married?

I just know. The glow settled itself in the notch between the two branches. *You don't have to, you know. You can just say no.*

I can?

Sure. Nobody ever has to do anything. They can always say no.

But my parents chose Joseph for me. They know me. They do what's best for me.

Yes, they do.

Mary was silent for a moment. The glowing thing in the tree was hard to see; she couldn't tell if it was a person who had a body like hers.

Even Elizabeth's parents chose for her. And she was old. Mary just barely remembered her cousin Elizabeth's wedding.

Yes. By the way, I have a secret about Elizabeth.

A secret?

Yes. She's going to have a baby.

Elizabeth? But she can't have babies! She's been married for so long and no baby ever came.

Well, she's having one now. I have another secret.

You do?

Yes.

Well, what is it?

You're going to have one, too.

Well, I hope so! At least one! More than that, I hope. I always tell people I'm going to have thirty-seven.

Well, I only know about the One.

Really? Mary wasn't sure whether or not to believe Gabriel, but she day-dreamed about babies all the time. *Boy or girl?*

Boy.

Oh. Mary wanted a girl, but that was all right. She could have a girl next time. Surely a few of the thirty-seven babies would be girls. Besides, where Mary lived, people always wanted to have a boy first. Probably Joseph would want a boy.

Do you know Joseph, too?

Yes. I come to him in dreams.

Not trees?

I come to you in trees.

You're pretty funny. Mary leaned closer to the glow. *What is Joseph like?*

He is a good man. He is quiet and gentle. He is strong. He will be good to you

Well, is he handsome?

I think you're all beautiful. But I came to talk about the baby.

What baby?

The one you're going to have. This is happening soon, Mary. Not years from now, but now.

Now? I'm thirteen!

Your little boy is going to be like other little boys, but also not like them. You will know this as soon as he is born, although you won't understand what it means for years. Things will happen throughout his life that will let you know that he is different.

Like what?

You will know. Stay alert and you will see.

But I don't see. Different how?

You're all God's children. But this baby will be the Son of God. And you will be His mother.

The Son of God?

He'll be the king.

Like King Herod? No, thanks. King Herod was a terrible king.

Nothing like King Herod. Your baby will be like no other person who has ever lived.

So this is why I'm getting married now? But you said I didn't have to get married. If I'm going to have a baby, hadn't I'd better hurry up?

You don't have to do any of this, Mary Gabriel said. *You can always say no. Or . . . you can be part of God's adventure.*

Mary thought. She thought of her mother at her age, setting off on the same path with Mary's father. She thought of Elizabeth, wishing for a baby and never having one, and how she was going to have one now. That was strange. She thought of this old tree, her companion throughout childhood, and that nothing glowing had ever sat in it and talked to her before. She thought of a baby boy, when she wanted a girl, and she felt the tiniest bit of excitement begin. She would go to Bethlehem. She would meet Joseph's sisters. She would see things she had never seen. Joseph was kind. Joseph had big hands, strong hands from being a carpenter. Gabriel was an angel. Her baby was a king, wearing a crown. . . .

"Miss Mary, are you ever coming in to help me with supper?" It was her mother. "I knew you'd fallen asleep out here!"

Mary looked up in the tree. It was empty. The sun was almost down, and the lamps were lit inside. Yes, she said in her mind, not with her lips. Yes. I'll do it. I'll be part of the adventure. Be it to me according to thy will.

Mary didn't tell
her second secret

A Conversation in the Kitchen

MARY WAS EXCITED. She slapped the soft balls of bread dough on the wooden table hard, over and over, until they were flat, then placed each one on the stone in the middle of the cooking fire.

"You mad at that bread?" her mother asked.

"Nope." Mary went on slapping the bread. They worked in silence for a few minutes, the only sound the slapping of the dough against the wooden table.

Finally Mary said, "I know a secret."

"You do?" Anna regarded Mary with amusement. This child had always been a caution. Anna never knew what she would come up with next. "And what might that be?"

"Secret."

"From your own mother? That must be some secret."

"Two secrets, actually."

"Oh, two secrets, is it?" Anna was finished chopping vegetables. She put them into the big old iron pot that she used for everything. "Two more loaves and then I need to put this on, all right?" They needed a bigger kitchen, she thought for the thousandth time. It was hard for two women to cook in there together. But of course, Mary would be leaving soon. So there would be only one woman cooking in the kitchen. Anna had a secret, too: she didn't want Mary to leave. She wanted her to stay home forever. But she would never tell her that. Not get married! What an idea.

"Yup." Mary scraped the last bit of dough out of the bowl and slapped it onto the tabletop. "Want a hint?"

"Yes, give me a hint."

"Elizabeth."

"Elizabeth? Well, she was here just a month ago—if she had a secret, don't you think I would know it?"

"Not if it's a secret, Mama."

"Ah. Of course. Let me see: Elizabeth found a golden coin in the street and is now a rich lady."

"No."

"All right: Elizabeth is going to become a dancing girl at the palace."

Mary laughed. Elizabeth was almost as old as Mama, and seemed older. She moved very slowly, and often complained about her back. "No."

"Zechariah has bought Elizabeth her own elephant."

"Mama, this is a real secret!"

"Well, all right, Miss. Why don't you just tell me?"

Mary dropped her voice to a whisper. "Elizabeth is going to have a baby."

Her mother straightened up and looked disapproving. "That's not very funny, Mary. You know she can't have a baby. Don't ridicule her for something she can't help."

Mary was indignant. "I'm not ridiculing her. It's the truth. She really is going to have a baby!"

"I don't think so, sweet. That would be so nice for her, but she's too old now.

It's just too late. Poor thing." Mama held a cup under the tap on the oil jar and opened it. A golden stream of olive oil poured into the cup. She replaced the cork. "You're the one who's going to have all the babies, remember? You and your thirty-seven babies?"

Mary didn't tell her mother her second secret.

"Mama, let's go see her tomorrow and find out. Can we go? We can wash the clothes early and set them out in the sun and go while they're drying, can't we? I can make more bread after supper and we can leave it for Papa's lunch, can't we? We haven't gone to see Elizabeth for a long time. And now that I'm getting married, maybe I won't be seeing her as much. Let's go tomorrow, please?"

"Mary, there's nothing to find out. I don't know where you get your ideas." Mama poured the oil into the iron pot and reached in with both hands to mix everything together.

"That's so disgusting." Mary said. "How can you do that?"

"That's the only way you know it's mixed. By hand. Next time you're going to mix it."

Suddenly Mary's stomach didn't feel well. That was strange. Mary was never ill. She gripped the edge of the table until it passed. Anna hadn't noticed.

"So, can we go?"

"Tomorrow?" Anna paused. "Well, maybe. I'll talk to your father when he comes in. Make the extra bread, anyway."

Mary smiled. She knew her father would say yes. She went over to the big crock of coarse wheat flour and measured out two cups. She got down the heavy stone mortar and pestle. She began to grind the wheat flour, a little at a time, until it was fine. They would go to Elizabeth's house in the next town. She would find out if the secret was true.

But somehow, she already knew it was.

My soul
proclaims
Your greatness
O my God
and my
spirit
has
rejoiced

The Visit

MARY AND HER MOTHER were up before daylight. The loaves of bread Mary had baked for her father's breakfast and lunch were on the table, together with some white goat cheese, a little dish of olives, and three fresh figs. Anna tied a few more loaves and figs up in a cloth for their own meal, and slung a leather bag of water over Mary's shoulder. "It'll be a picnic breakfast," she told her sleepy daughter.

Their footsteps sounded through the silent streets as they headed for the town gate. They met two or three women fetching the day's water from the town well, and saw lamplight in the windows of two or three houses, but almost everyone in town was still fast asleep. The black sky was turning to silver as they reached the gate, and then they were on the road.

It was still cold from the dark night, and they walked swiftly. Short, scrubby trees and large rocks emerged from the semidarkness along the road, and the hills to the West were still black and forbidding. They walked toward them, though, and as they walked, the first golden rays of the rising sun began to kiss the hills.

"Do you think the devil really lives in the West?" Mary asked her mother.

"You don't mean Elizabeth?"

Mary laughed out loud, surprising a bird, who flew suddenly up from her perch on a tree branch. "No, silly. The real devil. Do you think he really lives in the West?"

"No, I don't think so. That's just a story."

"And God lives in the East, where the sun comes up?"

"No. God lives everywhere."

"What do you think God looks like?"

"Well, how would I know? What do you think God looks like?"

"Golden," Mary said, remembering the tamarind tree. "Like fire, but not hot. Shining. Too shining to see clearly."

"Well, I guess we'll never know, will we?" said Anna. Mary could be an odd girl.

The sun was beginning to peek over the eastern horizon. "Some people think the sun is a god, you know," Mary told her mother.

"Well, some people aren't you," said Anna firmly.

"The Romans think that."

"The Romans think a lot of things. Let's have our breakfast when we get to that big tree at the bend in the road."

"Okay."

They were making good time. Soon they reached the tree, and Anna untied the cloth and spread it on the ground. Mary sat on a rock and pulled the cork out of the leather bag. She handed it to her mother, who drank from it, and then Mary took a long drink herself.

"We'll be there in time for a second breakfast," Mary said. "I hope Elizabeth has a lot of food."

"I just hope she's awake," Anna replied. Elizabeth was always talking about how tired she was. She took a long nap every afternoon, and sometimes one in the morning as well. She had a serving woman who cleaned her house and fetched her water. Mary wasn't sure what Elizabeth did all day. She had never known Anna to take a nap, not ever.

"I suppose Joanna will take care of the baby for her," Mary said, thinking out loud.

"There's no baby, Mary. I don't know where you get your ideas."

"Bet?"

"Bet what?"

"If there is no baby, I have to wash and braid your hair with my new ribbon."

"I wouldn't take your new ribbon."

"It's a bet, Mama."

"Well, it's a silly one, because there's no baby. Honey, Elizabeth is almost as old as I am."

"And if there is a baby?"

"There isn't," Anna said again.

"If there is a baby, you have to let me see Joseph."

Anna was shocked. "You can't see each other before you're married!"

"He doesn't have to see me. I just want to see what he looks like."

"He looks very nice."

"But I want to see him. And if Elizabeth is going to have a baby, you have to find a way to let me see him."

"Well, she's not," Anna said flatly. She got to her feet, picked up the picnic cloth, and shook it. "So it's a bet. And you won't see Joseph until it's time for you to see him. Which will be soon enough, Miss."

The sun was up now, and the road was bright. Birds sang to one another from the little trees, and here and there a tiny lizard darted from underneath one rock to another. After half an hour, they could see the wall of Elizabeth's town. Another half hour, and they were at the gate, and soon they reached Elizabeth's house. The serving woman Joanna sat on a bench outside the door, grinding dried chickpeas in a mortar.

"Well, well! Look who's here! Come in, come in. Put your bags down and let's get you ladies something to eat." Joanna was round and jolly, with a snow-white braid of hair almost down to her waist. She waddled inside ahead of Mary and Anna. "Oh, yes, I was just thinking of having a little something myself. What do you say to some dried fish?"

A wave of queasiness came over Mary at the very thought of dried fish. That was strange—the same thing had happened to her yesterday in the kitchen. Very odd.

"Maybe just some water, thanks, Joanna," she said.

"We ate along the road," Anna said. "And where is your lady?"

"Ah, still sleeping. She's very tired these days, let me tell you. Oh, yes, she is. And her back, of course. Oh, yes. But we women know all about that. Oh, yes. At times like this, very tired. Very, very tired. Oh, yes."

Mary stopped in her tracks. "Times like this?"

"Oh, yes. With a baby coming. Oh, yes. Her back. Oh my, yes."

"A baby." Mary darted a triumphant look at her mother, whose eyes were round with disbelief.

"Um, Elizabeth is having a baby?" Anna's voice was a whisper.

"Oh, yes. Oh my, yes. The town is talking, let me tell you. I imagine they're talking about it all the way in Rome. Oh my, yes."

"Having a baby—herself?"

Joanna shook with laughter. She never laughed out loud. She just shook like that, and you knew she was laughing. "Oh my, yes, herself." She lowered her voice and leaned toward Anna. "And at her age, let me tell you. Oh my, yes. They're talking, let me tell you."

"Joanna!" a thin voice came from the back of the house. "Help me get up!"

"Yes, Miss. Your cousins are here to see you, Miss. Oh, yes, I'm coming. And how are we this morning?" She padded off.

Mary and Anna were alone in the kitchen. "I don't believe it," said Anna. "It can't be."

"Shh!" said Mary. There was a shuffle in the hallway, and Elizabeth appeared, leaning on Joanna's stout arm. She was taller than Anna, and very thin, with hooded gray eyes. Her hair was gray, too, and had been since she was in her twenties. Mary eyed her belly intently. There was a definite roundness underneath her cousin's gown.

Joanna deposited her mistress in a chair. Elizabeth sighed and held out both feet. Joanna slid a footstool underneath them. Elizabeth dropped them heavily onto it, sighing again. "Oh, my back!"

Elizabeth never said hello. Never. She always said, "Oh, my back!" instead.

"Hello, dear. It seems that congratulations are in order," Anna said.

"Why I wanted to have a baby is beyond me. What was I thinking? The pain—you have no idea."

"I've had five children, Elizabeth."

"But I'm so much weaker than other people."

"You'll do fine. It probably wouldn't hurt you to walk a bit. Might help that back."

"Walk? I can barely move. You have no idea. This is God's doing."

"God is so good."

"Oh, my back! You have no idea."

"Cousin," Mary said, coming forward and touching Elizabeth's arm gently. "How did you know you were going to have this baby?"

Elizabeth looked at Mary and sighed. "Never mind."

"No, tell me. How did you know?"

"This you won't believe, Miss Mary," Elizabeth responded. "This you won't believe. I had a dream about you. I think it was a dream. Well, I'm not sure it was a dream. I was up in the night—my back, you know, it's so bad at night—keeps me up half the night. And I saw an angel, all golden. Only I dreamed it was you who was having a baby, not me. And you came to see me, just like today. And I told you that the angel said your baby was blessed and you were blessed, and that I was honored that you came to see me because you were the blessed baby's mother. Then I asked him about my back and he disappeared." Anna hid a smirk.

Elizabeth went on. "And not long after that—this," she gestured at her round belly. "That's it."

"He was—golden?"

"Yes."

"Did he . . . move, like?" Mary was remembering the tamarind tree again, and the way the golden light had shimmered and moved.

"Child, I don't remember. It was the middle of the night. My back was killing me."

"Is it hurting now?"

"You have no idea."

"Poor miss, let me give your back a good rub," said Joanna, "while Miss Anna makes you some nice ginger tea. It'll help your back, let me tell you. Oh my, yes. Miss Mary, go out into the garden and pull up a ginger root."

Mary hurried out the back door into the little walled garden. She looked up into the fruit trees, but there was no golden form to be seen. Still, she was excited. It was true. Elizabeth was having a baby. That meant that something was happening to her, too—she was sure. The adventure had begun.

Mary plucked a few weeds from around the ginger plants and pulled up a gnarly ginger root. She rapped it against the pavement to shake off the dirt. She was humming a tune, and began to sing as she headed back into the house.

My soul proclaims your greatness, O my God,
and my spirit has rejoiced in my salvation.
For you have looked with favor on your lowly servant.
From this day, all generations will call me blessed.
You, Almighty, have done great things for me,
and holy is your Name.
You have mercy on those who fear you, in every generation.
You have shown the strength of your arm.
You have scattered the proud in their conceit.
You have cast down the mighty from their thrones,
and have lifted up the lowly.
You have filled the hungry with good things,
and the rich you have sent away empty.
You have come to the help of your servant Israel,
for you have remembered your promise of mercy,
the promise you made to our forebears,
to Abraham and his children forever.

There was a miracle here

The Visit Continues—
The Sojourn Begins

FOR SOMEONE AS WEAK and ill as Elizabeth proclaimed herself to be, she ate a hearty meal: eggplant cooked with garlic and olive oil, an entire flat loaf of pita, several spoonfuls of nuts and raisins in rosewater, three or four slices of cold roasted lamb, and some little dried fish. She drank cup after cup of honey tea as she ate, and finished her breakfast with most of a plate of dates.

"I have to force it down, you know," Elizabeth said in her thin voice. "I'm eating for two now, you know."

"Oh my, yes," Joanna agreed, pouring her mistress and herself another cup of tea. Her plate was piled high with food, too, Mary noticed. Maybe everybody in this house was having a baby.

Mary and Anna ate, too, only not as much. Elizabeth always had wonderful food at her house, and plenty of it. Zechariah was a priest, and people were constantly giving him delicacies to take home. Mary reached for a second date, before Elizabeth and Joanna ate them all.

"You have no idea," Elizabeth was saying to Anna. "This child is kicking me to death this morning! To death! I'm black and blue inside, I know it. Maybe I shouldn't be sitting up. Joanna, I'll be having the rest of my meals in bed today. Just sitting up to eat this little bit of food has tired me out completely."

"Elizabeth, you'd do better to take a little walk around the garden. You don't want to grow weak from inactivity."

"Weak! But that's what I am. I'm so weak."

"Well, if you're going to have a baby, you'd better get strong. Mary, take Elizabeth out for a little walk. Elizabeth, go with Mary. Joanna and I will clean up here."

People usually did what Anna said. Mary took Elizabeth's bony arm and led her to the door and out into the garden, murmuring comforts and encouragements as they walked across the stone courtyard and set out along the wall.

"I don't know what it is about you, Mary," Elizabeth said with a slight groan. "Every time you come near me this child just about kicks me to death."

"Maybe he likes me." Maybe he knows the secret, Mary said to herself. Maybe babies know things we don't know.

"I just don't know how I'm going to manage," Elizabeth said. "I just don't know." Mary thought Elizabeth should manage just fine. She never did housework and she never cooked. She never sewed or spun or wove cloth. She never went to market. She never worked in the garden or fed the goat. Joanna did everything. She'd take care of the baby, too. Elizabeth would probably find a way for Joanna to give birth for her.

"Think of the work." Elisabeth sighed heavily. "I just don't know what we're going to do."

"You'll be all right," Mary said. "You'll do fine. You'll be such a good mother." Mary hoped God wasn't listening too hard, because that last sentence hadn't been completely sincere. "What a blessing you'll have!"

"Ugh!" Elisabeth grunted. "Did you see that? You could see my belly move, he kicked me so hard. I know it's a boy, I just know it. A girl wouldn't kick that hard."

Mary felt a funny flutter in her own belly. Not the queasy feeling, like before. And not a pain, not a pain at all. Just a little flutter, like butterflies' wings. She had never felt such a feeling before. It was such a nice feeling.

"Like butterflies," she said out loud.

"Butterflies, indeed!" Elizabeth said. "More like a camel! Oof! There he goes again."

"No, I meant me. I felt a little fluttering in my own belly just now."

"Well, you'll be feeling more than fluttering when your time comes, let me tell you. You have no idea. But when I dreamed about you and your baby, you were just as calm as anything. And the angel said you were blessed, and your baby was blessed. I wish *this* baby was blessed, so he wouldn't kick me half to death."

"I want to know more about your dream, if it was a dream," Mary said. "And about your baby. About how it happened. About the angel. Because—"

Anna came into the garden, carrying a large, flat basket of beans. "Feeling a little better?" she asked Elizabeth, crossing the pavement. She sat down on a bench in the shade and began to shell the beans, tossing the pods into the compost heap in the corner of the wall.

"Exhausted. Just exhausted." But Elizabeth looked better, no matter what she said. The walk had put some color into her thin cheeks, and her step was as almost as quick as Mary's.

"Well, the walk has done you good. You need to walk several times a day. Build up your legs and strengthen your back. Hanging clothes wouldn't hurt you. Gives you a good stretch."

"In my condition?"

"Oh, but it's so important, Elizabeth." Anna leaned forward over the basket of beans and looked serious. Only Mary could tell when Anna was joking sometimes.

"If you're too weak to have the baby in the normal way, do you know what happens?"

"What?" Elizabeth breathed.

"They cut you open and take it out."

Elizabeth gave a little scream.

"They did that to the emperor. Cut his mother open and took him right out. They did that because his mother didn't take enough walks beforehand."

Elizabeth put one hand on her round belly and sat down. Mary rolled her eyes.

"Truth." Anna bent down and plucked a bay leaf off the bush beside the step. "Walk every day, several times a day. And have Joanna bring the clothes to you and you hang them on the bushes yourself. Good stretch. And maybe do some sweeping in the house. Good exercise for the stomach and back. Make you strong. So they don't have to cut you open."

Elizabeth gave a little whimper. "Oh, my back!"

"Maybe I can stay with you for a little while, Elizabeth. We can take walks together until you get used to it. I could help Joanna put the spring vegetables in—you don't have any in yet, and soon it will be too hot. I could help you sew for the baby—you're going to need lots of things for him." Mary wanted to learn more about Elizabeth's dream. Somehow, the two of them were together in the angel's errand. Related. Something was going on. "Couldn't I stay for a while, Mama? Joanna could walk you home and then Papa could come for me in a few weeks. I could help out here until Elizabeth feels stronger." Mary believed that Elizabeth was strong as a horse, but she needed time to find out about the dreams and the baby.

"Stay here?" Anna was puzzled. Mary had been teary-eyed yesterday evening about leaving home and now she wanted to stay with whining Elizabeth for weeks. Girls were so fickle. "Well, I suppose you could stay here for a little while. I need to get home, though. There's nobody to take care of your father."

Thus it was decided. Anna and Joanna set off the next morning, leaving Mary and Elizabeth already out in the garden, draping wet laundry over the bushes to dry in the sun. Elizabeth was beginning to take charge, explaining to Mary just how each piece should be hung, as if Mary had never done laundry before. This might be a long visit, Mary thought as she listened patiently. But there was a miracle in this house, and Mary was hot on the trail of another one. She would find out what Elizabeth knew and what she had been told. She would read between the lines. She would ponder. The fluttering in her belly was happening so often now that she had almost stopped noticing it. But she was beginning to suspect that it was not butterflies.

ജ⚬ഇ

Joseph pushed his old plane along the white surface of a long plank of oak, shaving off a curl of wood that twirled around and around itself. He shaved another, and another, until the whole surface of the plank was smooth and the floor was covered with paper-thin spirals of wood. Then he lifted the plank off the worktable and stacked it with the others just like it. This would be a tabletop. The legs were already done—thick posts of the same heavy oak, almost as thick as the tree from which he had cut them. That tree would make two tables, he was sure—maybe three. It was a big one.

Make straight in the desert a highway for our God. Joseph thought of that verse every time he planed wood: that's exactly what happens in planing wood, he thought to himself. All the rough places are made smooth, and the bumps straightened out. Flat and smooth. Beautiful, like life should be.

And why shouldn't life be beautiful? Why shouldn't there be joy in life? Every time you take a new piece of wood, you start something new. You get a second chance every time. If things don't work out with one piece of wood, you go and get another one and you try again. That's the way it is in carpentry. Why shouldn't it be that way in other places?

His son was chopping at what remained of the tree outside the shop. Probably Joseph would let James plane the next one, to give him some practice. Planing takes a lot of practice before you get to be any good, to where the thin curls of wood rise up off the board just right as you go along. At first, you keep angling it wrong and digging into the board, making dents and ruts where you should have a smooth, uneventful white surface. Only one way to learn. James was a good boy, and he would be a good carpenter. Big hands, like Joseph's hands. You need big hands.

Joseph wondered what Mary's hands were like. Small, certainly. She was young. Strong, though: you don't have to be big to be strong. Each of us is strong in our own way, he thought, setting the next board in the groove on the work table and picking up the plane again.

Yes, she cooks as well as her mother, Joachim had said as the two men drank tea together. Bakes all the bread we eat and has since she was a tiny little thing. And amiable, too. Even funny—we laugh all the time at her. But never disrespectful, he had hastened to add. Sings like an angel, Mary does. Sings around the house like a little bird.

A woman singing around the house again. Fresh, hot bread at supper. Someone to talk to at night. Amiable, her father said. Even funny. Joseph smiled a little to himself, and a curl of wood came up perfectly off the board.

And they saw each other.

The Table

Life with Elizabeth was about what Mary had expected it would be. She was able to persuade her cousin to become a little more active: they hung clothes together on the bushes, walked in the walled courtyard together, and gardened together, which meant that Elizabeth planted one onion set, and then watched while Mary put in the other ninety-nine. Joanna continued to do all the housekeeping, which meant that Mary wasn't working nearly as hard at Elizabeth's house as she usually did at her own. At home, Mary and Anna did all the housework together, and it occupied most of every day. Here, Mary had time on her hands.

She did learn the complete story of Elizabeth's unusual pregnancy. How Zechariah hadn't believed the angel when the baby was promised, and was struck dumb for his disbelief. Now he was having to write on a tablet every time he wanted to say something. So now, rather than teaching and greeting people as he usually did as a senior priest, he was managing the actual sacrifices. The primary means of worship was the sacrifice of animals: they slit their throats and poured the blood on the altar, then cooked the meat in great metal pans. Blood was everywhere, and the smell was awful. Incense would be piled onto every fire of animal flesh, but it never conquered the reek of the sacrificial smoke. Zechariah was away right now, taking his turn and then someone else's in this grisly business. He would return at the end of the month in a foul mood, with a bag full of bloody vestments for Joanna to wash clean.

"And so Zechariah's at the Temple all day, week after week, while I suffer here alone," Elizabeth said, helping herself to another fig at lunch. Mary had been with her for almost three months. Elizabeth was now quite round in the belly, and looked to be in fine health: pink cheeks, bright eyes. She was never sick to her stomach, and seemed to have a limitless appetite, but none of these happy facts interfered in the slightest with her complaining.

"But you're going to have a baby. Surely that must make you happy."

"I was happy before."

Mary couldn't remember Elizabeth ever having been what anyone would call happy.

"Well, anyway, what shall we do today?" Mary said, hoping to get Elizabeth's mind off her troubles. "We have the mint bed to clean up—it's already overgrown. And we could put in more eggplants, because we still have some plants from Mama. And Mama said to be sure and cut the hyssop right as it blooms, for the best tea, because that's what you'll need when the baby comes."

"I feel so weak. I'm too weak to garden, I know it. I'd faint for certain."

"Well, then, sit outside with me while I cut back the mint and get the hyssop. You can pull the mint leaves off the stems and we'll dry them flat."

Mary installed Elizabeth in her chair out in the garden, and went back into the house to fetch the large flat herb basket. Before she could return to the garden, though, there was a heavy knock on the door to the street. Joanna usually answered the door, but she was at the market. Mary set down her basket and fastened her scarf so that it covered the lower part of her face, then ran to the door and opened it.

There stood a man and a boy, each carrying one end of a large wooden table.

"Good morning, Miss," said the man. "Here is the table your master ordered, finished ahead of time."

Mary flushed with embarrassment. "Oh, I don't work here. Joanna is out right now. I'm just visiting. Zechariah is my cousin's husband. My cousin is in the garden. Shall I get her?"

The man started slightly, as if something had surprised him. "Oh, you're Elizabeth's cousin? The daughter of Anna and Joachim?" Mary had turned and started toward the back of the house, but she stopped and turned back.

"Um . . . yes. I'm Mary. And . . . whom shall I say is here? With the table?" Mary's heart was beating so loudly she thought for certain the man could hear it. This man was a carpenter. He knew her parents. He knew they had a daughter. Could he be. . . ?

"My name is Joseph." His voice, which had been so pleasantly rich and rumbly, was suddenly strained. Suddenly he was looking down at his table top. His son was watching him, bewildered.

"Oh." Mary's eyes were downcast, too. The table top gleamed. Their faces were reflected in it, two people looking down, a bearded man and a veiled woman. They saw each other in the reflection at the same instant, and quickly lifted their eyes from the table top, only to find them locked on each other in the flesh.

"You are Mary." His brown eyes searched hers.

"Oh," Mary said again. She could feel her cheeks turn pink. She wished she didn't blush so easily. She became aware of the boy watching them both with open curiosity, and she quickly looked back down at the table.

"Oh, forgive me. Won't you come in?" She couldn't just leave them standing there at the door. Where were her manners?

"Thank you, Miss Mary." Joseph and his son picked up the heavy table and turned it sideways until it could go through the door. Carefully they guided it through without knocking against the doorpost even once.

"It's beautiful," Mary said, stroking the gleaming table top that had so recently caught them both in such a surprising truth. "So smooth."

"All from the wood of one tree," Joseph said proudly. "And the legs are just about as big around as the trunk. This table will last a long, long time, Miss Mary. It will last until you are an old lady; it will last until your great-great-great-granddaughter is an old lady. It will last longer than that. Long, long after you and I have both died."

"I can't imagine being so old. Or dying."

"That's because you are so young now. Life moves very quickly once it gets going."

Mary lifted her eyes to his again. "Yes," she said, "it certainly does."

Footsteps sounded in the hallway, and Elizabeth appeared at the door. "Oh, my poor back! I was wondering what had happened to you, girl. Oh, hello, Joseph—I see the table's finished. Well, bring it into the kitchen, then, and move the old one out to the courtyard. I don't know what's keeping Joanna. She knows I have to have my tea in the midmorning, to keep my strength up. I think I'd better just go back to bed. Mary, show him where it should go, that's a good girl. Oh, my back!" If Elizabeth had any qualms about leaving Mary and Joseph together, she gave no sign of it.

The new table was brought in, and the old one set against the wall outside. Mary made Joseph and James sit down and brought them big cups of cool water with slices of lemons and tiny fresh green mint leaves floating in them, and a plate of dates. Nobody spoke much; Mary and Joseph kept meeting each other's eyes and then looking away in embarrassment.

Then Joseph spoke. "I'll be seeing your father again after the Sabbath, when your parents come to get you."

"Mama and Papa are coming to get me now?" Mary had lost track of the time she had spent with Elizabeth.

"Yes. We'll be talking then. You know that I must go to Bethlehem?"

Mary nodded.

"And that my family must be counted?" Suddenly Joseph seemed less confident and self-assured.

Mary nodded again, not trusting herself to speak.

"So—well—you'll be in my family, then?"

Mary looked down and nodded again.

His name is John

A Baby and a Journey

MARY LIFTED A DRIPPING CLOTH out of the water and wrung it hard. Then she opened it and placed it gently onto the rosemary bushes. The garden looked like a miniature field of cotton, each of the bushes lifting something white toward the hot sun. Everything would be dry in half an hour.

Two more months had passed. Mary and her parents were back again to help with Elizabeth. As she hung the laundry, Mary kept one ear attuned to the goings-on inside—deafening shrieks issued regularly from the room where Elizabeth and Zechariah slept. Elizabeth was having her baby.

"Oh, Miss! Oh, my! Just breathe! Oh, yes! Oh, yes! Just breathe, now! Oh, yes, there you go, just breathe like a good girl." Joanna's voice was as calm as Joanna's voice could be, but it was a loud voice under the best of circumstances. Mary went back inside with the empty laundry basket.

"Let me lift you up a little, Elizabeth," Anna said, "Just sit up a bit. It's really better to do it sitting up. It's almost time."

Elizabeth flopped back down on her array of pillows and screamed loud enough to wake the dead. "I can't get up."

"Here we go," said Anna, ignoring her and gesturing to Mary to take Elizabeth's other arm. Mary put down her laundry basket. Together they lifted Elizabeth into a kneeling position, while Joanna knelt in front of her and held her shoulders. Joanna was like a small mountain, and within seconds Elizabeth was holding onto Joanna's shoulders and pulling against her for all she was worth. She had stopped screaming about what she couldn't do, or about anything at all. The groans of her great effort were answered by encouraging shouts from the other women. "Here he comes! Here's his head! He has lots of hair, Elizabeth! One more push! And just one more!"

A thin cry came from the new arrival and a final groan from Elizabeth, who collapsed on the bed. Mary wiped the tiny face clean with one finger wrapped in a cloth, while Anna and Joanna busied themselves with the cord. Then they plopped the baby on Elizabeth's chest, where he immediately began searching for something to eat. His mother smiled, quiet for once, and Anna settled a soft blanket over the two of them.

⚭

Joachim hadn't come along with his family just for the blessed event. He had also to make final arrangements with Joseph for the impending marriage. All the men were sitting on the bench in front of the house when Anna came out with the news of the baby's birth. Joachim slapped old Zechariah on the back.

"Well, what's the baby's name?" Joseph asked, handing Zechariah his tablet. Zechariah still couldn't speak.

But now the old man cleared his throat. "His name is John," he croaked, and cleared his throat again. "John," he said again, shaking his head in wonder, and got up and went slowly into the house to see his wife and his first child, leaving the others outside.

They hadn't been talking about babies. They had been talking about taxes. And the strange Roman idea of a census. Why did it matter to the Romans exactly how many people there were in Judea? Why did they want to know? Why weren't our own temple records enough, and people's own testimony about their families? Most things the Romans did turned out badly for Israel one way or another; this one would be, at the very least, a monumental inconvenience for every Jewish family.

"Who will watch my shop while I'm off getting myself counted?" Joseph asked no one in particular. "Why can't they take my word for it that I'm getting married? Something is very strange about this whole matter."

"I believe they are doing it because they can," Joachim said thoughtfully. "I believe they think it's a good idea to keep us mindful of their power to make us do things we don't want to do. I think they want to keep us a little afraid, all the time."

"And they want our money," Joseph said. "We'll see a tax on each family member within the year after they're finished with this count. Mark my words. They want us not to get married and have children. They think we won't if they tax each one of us. I think they're secretly afraid of us if we grow too numerous and too strong."

"Well, my dear son," said Joachim with a smile, "any second thoughts, then? Can you afford to marry my daughter? She'll cost you more money, and you'll have more children. Lots more, if God is good. More money to the Romans. Not backing out now, are you?"

"No, my noble father, I am not backing out. I'll just make more money. James and I will build more houses and make more furniture, and then all the little ones who come along will help us and we'll make even more. There won't be a person in town who doesn't live in one of my houses. I'll be so rich, your daughter won't be able to count the number of her servants."

"That's all right. Let the Romans count them. And when are you building me a new house? Your dear father-in-law?"

"Well, I'll need to add another room to my house, for all my gold. So I'll let you know."

Joachim was silent for a moment. Then he spoke.

"When do you leave?"

"At once, really. I must be there before the end of their year, they say. I don't know how long it will take once we arrive, and it's a long journey."

"You are walking, of course."

"Of course, I am walking. And James is walking. And your daughter is riding."

"Riding? On what?"

"Do you think I'm going to let my new wife walk along in the dust for weeks? I bought her a little donkey, and she is waiting for a name and a lovely little mistress."

Joachim's eyes filled with sudden tears. "That's nice," he said. "Nice. You take good care of our girl, now."

"I will. You know I will. And we'll be back very soon—as soon as we can." Joseph put one hand on Joachim's shoulder. "She'll be just a morning's walk away."

Laughter and the clatter of dishes sounded from inside, and the men got up and entered the house. Joachim was seated at the new table with Anna, a large array of food spread out before him. Joanna was padding back and forth from the cupboard with dish after dish, while Mary folded dry clothes. Occasionally there was a little cry from the back room, and one of the women would run back to see if all was well. All was surprisingly well—not a complaint had been heard from Elizabeth since the baby's birth. More food was brought, the new table admired, the miracle of Zechariah's voice remarked again and again.

Twice Mary went into the back room and came back with the baby for the men to admire. Neighbors came and went until well after dark, and finally it was time to sleep. Mary, Joseph, and James had a journey ahead of them.

And in the morning, before the roosters of the town had awakened, Joanna was up, packing an immense basket of food for the travelers. Elizabeth lay in bed with the baby, who had already finished his breakfast and gone back to sleep. Mary and Anna and Joachim sat on the bench outside waiting for Joseph.

Mary was dressed warmly against the cold of the early morning, the cloak her mother had made her wrapped tightly around her body. She leaned against her mother on the bench in the dark, and Anna held her in both arms.

"You'll be safe. Keep warm, though."

"I will."

"He is such a good man."

"Yes, he is. He's funny, too."

"Like you. I wanted you to have a funny one."

"Papa's funny, too."

"Yes. We're all funny. All thirty-seven of your babies will be funny, too— just wait."

Mary thought of the fluttering in her belly. She thought of its new hardness that nobody knew about. Nobody knew about this, not even her mother, not even Joseph, but somehow she was not worried about any of it.

"I don't think about thirty-seven anymore, Mama," she said. "I'm thinking about one right now."

"One at a time. We do every thing one at a time. Every day, one at a time."

The clip-clop of hooves sounded on the street. Joseph and James were coming.

"Be good, girl," Joachim said, hugging Mary and Anna together.

"I will, Papa."

"One day at a time, Mary," Anna said, fighting back tears.

"Yes, Mama." Mary had given up fighting; the tears ran down her cheeks.

Joseph lifted Mary up onto the donkey's back, took Mary's bundle from Anna, and kissed Joachim on both cheeks. He nodded to Anna and smiled.

"We'll be very careful. We'll be back as soon as we can. I'll send word if I meet anyone you know."

Anna reached up and placed her hand on Mary's forehead. "God bless you in His Holy Name," she said. James picked up the lead and began to walk, with Joseph walking beside the donkey to steady Mary and all their bundles. Joachim and Anna watched them as they walked away, and stood on the doorstep until they couldn't see them any more. The sun was just beginning to rise in the East.

she took one
of his hands
and placed it
on her belly.

A Journey and a Story

Mary had no plan about how to tell Joseph her news. They had never been alone together, until now. They weren't even alone now—James was with them. But the trip would be a long one, and she would have abundant time to tell him about the thing that had happened to her in the garden—and everything that had been happening since. For no rational reason, she was not afraid to tell him, even though she knew that her news would shock him. Or would it? Joseph did not seem to be the kind who is easily shocked. She would just have to wait and see.

The sun was fully up as they made their way out of the town and up into the hills. It would be a fine day, a day of blue sky and bright sunlight. They would walk until the sun was high above them and then stop for rest and food.

"I can walk, you know," Mary said. "Any time you want me to, I can take a turn walking and you or James can ride. I'm very strong."

Joseph laughed. "Maybe James. Not me. What do you say, James?"

"Not me," said the boy stoutly. He wasn't about to ride if his father didn't.

"Well, I am very strong," Mary said again. She didn't want Joseph to think for even a minute that she was anything like her cousin.

"Good for you, Miss. So your father tells me. And as good a cook as your mother."

"Well actually, I don't think I am. Not yet. But I love to cook and I love to see people eat."

"You're making me hungry," said James. "All this talk about food." James loved to eat. He could drink a pitcher of goat's milk all by himself at a meal, and he ate more than Joseph. James was growing.

"We'll walk to that far hill and then find a nice place to stop and rest. There'll be a stream for the donkey."

"What's the donkey's name?" asked Mary.

"Well, now, that's up to you, I'd say," said Joseph. "She's your donkey."

"You mean I get to name her myself?"

"It's only right."

Mary smiled. Then she laughed.

"I have an idea."

"And your idea is what?"

"I think I'd like to call her Elizabeth."

Joseph chuckled and his son hooted with laughter. Everyone in town knew Elizabeth.

"What a fine name."

"Elizabeth will never know."

"Never."

Elizabeth's hooves clip-clopped along. She was sure-footed over the rocky paths through the hills, and Joseph and James were strong enough to match her endurance. In an hour they had reached the far hill; a little stream ran down from its top and splashed into a pool at the bottom. Mary slid off the donkey and spread out her shawl to use as a picnic cloth, while James led Elizabeth to the stream, took off her saddle, and let her drink. Joanna's farewell basket was full of delicious things: little biscuits made from wine, goat cheese wrapped in grape leaves, some legs of roasted chicken, a comb of honey and at least a dozen flat loaves of bread.

Mary was starving. She ate one helping of everything and looked longingly at the one remaining chicken leg. She would leave it for James. Instead, she spread some honey on a piece of bread.

"Do you have chickens?" she asked Joseph.

"We used to," he said.

"My mother had so many chickens you wouldn't believe your eyes if you saw them all," James said. "She sold the eggs. Some days she had fifty eggs."

"Oh." Mary wasn't sure what to say. She was so curious about Joseph's first wife. Nobody spoke for a while.

"What, um—happened to her?" Mary asked Joseph at last.

"She died birthing James's little sister," Joseph said quietly. "She was turned around inside and the midwife couldn't turn her right in time."

"Was it . . . a long time ago?" Mary was embarrassed. Joseph had loved his wife, she could see. And he had lost a baby girl, too. It was so sad. But she also felt an unworthy feeling of jealousy. What a terrible person I am, she thought to herself.

"Almost ten years," Joseph said. "A long time for two men to be alone."

A wave of tenderness swept through Mary. "Now I can take care of you both," she said. "I'm young, but I know how to keep a house."

"We'll have good times," Joseph said, with a relaxed smile. "We need some good times. We need someone to sing around the house like a bird. Your father says you sing like a bird."

"Oh, I don't know. I like to sing." Mary was embarrassed again. "Maybe Elizabeth can sing with me. We can sing duets. Donkeys have such lovely voices."

James was off wading in the pool, holding his head under the stream of water and feeling it splash on him.

"You're a funny girl," Joseph said, looking at Mary's face. She flushed and looked down at her piece of bread. He reached out and took her chin in his hand, turning her face back toward him. "We'll be happy together." Then he took his hand away. He thought a moment. "I want you to know that I will come no closer to you than you wish, for as long as you wish. I know you are young. You're much younger than I am. I don't want you to be afraid of me. I'm just happy to have you in my family. I've been alone a long time. I can wait. I want you to be glad."

Mary's eyes filled with tears. This was a good man. Anna had been right. But what would he say when he knew her secret? This was his secret, too. It was time to tell him.

"Joseph," she began. Joseph smiled at the sound of his name on her lips. She had not spoken his name before.

"Joseph," she said again, and then she stopped. How to begin?

"Joseph, do you believe in God?"

"What a question, Mary," Joseph said. "Of course I do. Everyone believes in God."

"I mean, do you follow Him?" This was awful. She wasn't being at all clear. "I mean, would you do anything He asked you to do?"

"Well, yes," Joseph said "I'm not sure He's ever come right out and asked me to do anything. But if He did, I certainly would."

"Oh." Mary was quiet, playing with the fringe on her shawl. "Well, so would I."

"Good for you," Joseph said with a twinkle, trying to get a smile out of her. But he could see that something was wrong. "Mary, what is it? Are you afraid I'm not righteous enough?"

"Oh, no! That's not it at all! It's just that . . . something has happened to me." And then she told Joseph the whole story: the angel in the tamarind tree, the message about the baby and who the baby would become. The strange coincidence of Elizabeth's baby and Elizabeth's dream. The flutterings in her belly the last few months. Mary's belly was getting round, like Elizabeth's had been, and hard as a rock. It didn't even feel like it was hers. She had longed to ask Anna. Joanna. Even Elizabeth. Somebody.

"But I have told no one until right now. You are the first."

Joseph was silent. Mary did not look down at her hands, or play with the fringe on her shawl. She looked right into Joseph's eyes.

"The baby is coming. The time is now—soon. I have known this ever since that day. And no matter what you decide to do, I will give this baby life. You are a good man. You will decide rightly. I trust God and I trust you. I can do nothing else."

Still Joseph did not speak. He got up and walked the thirty paces to the road they had traveled, looking down across the valley to the next set of hills in the distance. Somewhere beyond those hills lay the city of Bethlehem and the graves of his forefathers. Behind him lay his home and the grave of his wife and child. In between, here beside the road, were Mary and his son James, everything for which he had hoped through all the lonely years of waiting. A family again. A wife. Singing like a bird through the house.

He could have Mary as she was, all she was, and he would never know fully what she was. And she would never know him fully. We do not know each other fully. And we do not know God, not fully. We are beyond each other, and God is beyond all of us.

And now, Mary's baby. A second son. A son of whom he was not the father. As Mary was not the mother of James. And yet she had cast her lot in with the two of them, pledging herself not just to Joseph but to the care of his son as well. She would make a home for both of them. She would not be his mother, but she would do her best, Joseph could tell. She could have said nothing, could have allowed him to think the child was his. Women did that all the time. But not this one.

He turned and walked back to her. She had risen to her feet and was watching him. Her lips trembled and tears ran down her cheek, but she paid no attention to them. She gazed at him steadily.

Slowly, Joseph held out his hand. As slowly, Mary took it. She brought his hand to her lips and kissed it, still gazing at him. Then he pulled her to him and surrounded her with his strong arms, arms that could swing an ax and fell a tree, arms that could lift a heavy load. She took one of his hands and placed it on her belly, so he could feel its roundness.

⊱⊙⊰

The trip was long. Mary was tired at the end of each day, more tired than she wanted either Joseph or James to know. The basket of provisions lasted only a few days, and then they had to buy food from farmers whose homes they passed, or from merchants along the way, or from shops in the little towns through which they traveled. Sometimes they slept under the stars, Mary curled up alongside Joseph under his heavy cloak, her head pillowed on his arm, James on the other side, with Elizabeth the donkey making snuffling noises as she slept. And sometimes they slept in the stables of hospitable families along the road.

The stables were underneath the houses here in the hills, for the most part: animals on the ground floor, a space carved right into the hillside, and the family up above. Travelers often slept with the animals, bringing their own animals inside along with those of their hosts. Joseph sometimes did a little work for a farmer before they set off again: repairing something, helping with a new fence, advising about the construction of a new piece of furniture. Mary would visit with the farmer's wife and help with chores while the men worked, and then there would be a meal to which they were invited. Afterward, everyone sat by the fire and told stories or sang songs until exhaustion sent them all to bed—Mary, Joseph, and James down below to sleep in the warm, sweet straw, and the family to their own sleeping quarters.

There were inns, of course. But staying with families was better. Robbers and soldiers frequented some of the inns, and Joseph did not know the area. Many people slept in one room in the inns, with strangers all together, and Mary needed her privacy now. In the straw, with the clouds of the animals' warm breath in the night, the little family was safe and warm.

They were getting close to Bethlehem. One of the families with whom they stayed was of the house of David, like Joseph, and he and James and the husband sat up late in the night, talking about the census and the Romans and the king, while Mary slept, exhausted, down in the stable in the straw, curled up against Elizabeth for warmth, her face buried in the donkey's shaggy coat. She hadn't felt like eating that night, she was so tired, and her back hurt like anything. She knew what that meant.

The baby would be coming soon.

How do they know what to do?

A Child Is Born

As weary and achy as Mary had been in the night, she was full of energy in the morning: up before Joseph and James, feeding Elizabeth, filling their leather bags with water for the rest of their journey. She missed cooking—not having your own kitchen is the worst part of traveling, she thought to herself. Much worse than sleeping in a stable, which she had actually come to enjoy. She wondered what the kitchen was like in Joseph's house. Would she be using the same pots and bowls Joseph's wife had used? Of course she would. What a foolish question. A pot is a pot.

The baby within her had long ago ceased his gentle flutters—he was kicking away enthusiastically now. Mary felt enormous: she could no longer see her own feet when she looked down. Gabriel had never mentioned that part.

There were so many things she hadn't known. The shocking hardness of her belly. That her navel would almost disappear. That she would waddle around like old Joanna. That she would need help getting on and off Elizabeth. Mary was used to running and climbing anywhere she chose. It was odd to have to stop and consider whether she could or could not do something. She had stopped offering to walk. Joseph and James had never taken her up on it, anyway.

There certainly were a lot of politically minded people in Joseph's family. They were meeting more and more of his relatives as they got nearer Bethlehem, and each evening, in each house, the men talked by the fire far into the night. Always the same topics: the census, the tax, the Romans. Some of the women sat and listened, but Mary was usually too tired to stay up. She had come to feel quite safe and at home with the animals, cuddling against Elizabeth's furry body until Joseph and James came down to bed at last. Then all four of them slept in a row, donkey and humans together on blankets over a thick layer of warm-smelling clean straw. It was a comfortable way to rest, though Mary had never expected it to be so. She wondered what her mother would think if she could see her. She wondered about it every night.

She thought her mother would like it just fine. She was like her mother, she thought: taking what came. Anna was like that, and Mary was like that, too. That's a good way to be. You can be surprised by things, but you don't have to be scared. Things don't have to be exactly what you expect.

"When will we be in Bethlehem?" James asked his father late one morning as they walked along a steep path up a hill.

"Tired of walking?" Joseph asked.

"No," James said quickly. "Just wondering."

"Well, we might reach there tomorrow by sundown. I think it's just beyond that row of hills. Or the one beyond that. If it's the next one, then I guess it'll be the day after tomorrow. We're almost there, though."

"Do they have stables under the houses?" Mary asked. She hoped so. She didn't want to have her baby at an inn, in front of soldiers.

"Some of the stables are for more than one house, maybe lots of houses," Joseph said. "People come and get their animals in the morning and bring them back in the evening. And lots of people there don't even own cows or sheep themselves. They buy milk and things from other people. Most of them do it that way."

Well, this would be different, thought Mary, a little uneasily. So many people in Bethlehem. So many more now, too, with all the families traveling there to be counted. They had been in the countryside up until now, or in tiny villages. The nights had been quiet. The people had been friendly. There had been women to talk with and children to play with. And the animals, of course—being in a stable had been the same thing as being with a family. This would be different. Maybe the baby would wait until they were finished with their business in Bethlehem, and they could get back on the road through the countryside. That would be good.

They got to town by sundown the next day. Bethlehem was noisy and full of a million smells: cooking food from a hundred kitchens, hot metal from the anvils of the blacksmiths, leather from the saddleries, spices from the shops along the street, the excrement of animals and people mixing in the gutter. The main street wound around through the town forever, it seemed, until Joseph stopped and studied one doorway.

"This may be my cousin's place," he said. "I'm not sure."

Mary sat up straighter on Elizabeth, so she didn't look like such a waif. She felt like a waif, though, or maybe like a pumpkin—she was so round now. Yes. She felt just like a pumpkin.

Joseph knocked and, after a moment, the door opened. A broad face peeked out from behind the heavy door. "Full up," said the face. "No room. Sorry."

"This is not the inn of Micah bar Eliezar?"

"Hasn't been for years. Micah's been dead for ten years. Maybe more."

"Ah. I didn't know. I am his father's cousin's son."

"My wife was married to Micah bar Eliezar. Now I have the inn."

"Ah. And the wife?"

The fat man laughed and opened the door wider. "And the wife! Ha! Yes, I have the wife, too! She came with the inn! Come out, Miriam, and see ... what did you say your name was?"

"Joseph ben Jacob. My wife is called Mary."

"Come out and meet your cousin Joseph!"

A gray-haired woman poked her head out of a nearby window. "Well, don't make them stand out in the street, you old fool. Where are your manners? Get that worthless boy up here to take the donkey downstairs. Mattias! Get up here this instant! He's a worthless boy, that one. Mattias! I'm going to kill you when you get up here, so hurry!"

Mary's heart leapt at the word "downstairs." This would be the stable. Under the house, just like out in the country. The four of them in the comfortable straw. Joseph lifted Mary onto the ground. Her legs buckled under her a bit. She was so tired.

"Hello, dear. Let's get you inside and give you a cup of tea." She caught a glimpse of Mary's belly. "Oho! Lord, Lord, look what we have here! A baby coming for sure. This very night, by the look of you, dear. Some tea. Bring you around for sure. Come along."

A boy about James's age appeared. He and James stared at each other for an instant, and then James handed him Elizabeth's lead and they all disappeared down the alley that led to the house's back entrance.

Joseph and their host went into the house and the two women followed, making their way to the kitchen. In no time the men were drinking tea together in the front room, while Mary and old Miriam sipped theirs at the large kitchen table.

"Seven children, I had, dear, and a terrible time with each one of them," Miriam said as she set little raisin cakes out on two plates. "Such pain! Tea is what you need, dear. Get you through it somehow. Oh, Lord, I never felt such pain as I felt with my first. He just about ripped me in half, that boy. Have a little cake, there's a good girl."

Suddenly Mary wasn't very hungry. She took one of the cakes and nibbled at the edge of it. "The first one is always the worst," Miriam was saying as she helped herself to another cake. "Oh, Lord! Forty-one hours hard labor—that was me with my first. You could hear me scream on the other side of town. And the blood! Oh, Lord. You should have seen the sheets. Bright red, they were, like I'd been in a war."

Mary put her raisin cake back on her plate. Even a war sounded pleasant compared to Miriam's description of childbirth.

Mary was so tired she could hardly see. And her back hurt, too, in aching waves below what had been her waist. "I think I'd like to rest, thank you," she said. "The tea was lovely."

"You'll need it, dear. That's all I can say. Rest while you can."

James and Matthias were down in the stable, playing a game with little smooth stones on the hard dirt floor. But James had already fixed their beds in the straw, and Elizabeth was already snuffling in her sleep beside the thick, high bundle upon which Mary would lie.

"Thanks, James," she said. "You are a truly great man."

"Sure am," James said. "Do you mind if we keep playing?"

"No, I like it. My brothers at home were always playing some kind of game while I was drifting off. Do you mind if I go to sleep?"

"If you don't snore."

"Well, how would I know if I do or not?"

"I'd wake you up and tell you."

Mary pulled the soft blanket over herself, poked and rearranged the straw under her sheet until it felt just right under her back. She stared at the ceiling. Elizabeth sighed, and Mary reached over and stroked her fuzzy flank. One of the older lambs nuzzled at its mother's belly, searching for a teat, and the mother gave a low bleat as she flopped over on her side. The pebbles fell again and again on the floor, as the boys commented softly on their game. Outside, the street noises continued: people walking by, people arguing, a drunken man singing, soldiers marching by on night patrol.

∽⚬∾

Hours must have passed when Mary jerked suddenly awake. Joseph was beside her now, and James was asleep on the other side of Elizabeth. Mattias was sleeping over in the corner of the room. The street outside was quiet.

But something was happening inside. The blanket beneath Mary was wet, and so was her skirt. A strong wave of pain passed through her back, like the clenching of a fist, and then it subsided. Another one. And another. This must be it.

The clenching felt better, Mary discovered after a few more, when she breathed hard out through her mouth in short little breaths, like the panting of a dog. But she would need to get up and do something about the mattress and the blanket and everything. What a mess.

She wanted her mother. But her mother wasn't there.

Somebody was, though. Something in the corner of the room shimmered and came closer. Something she had seen before.

Gabriel!

It's time now. Don't be afraid.

I'm trying not to be. But Mary was afraid. Terribly afraid. Suddenly it seemed clear that this wasn't going to work, that there was no way what was in her belly could ever escape. *I can't do this!* she wailed, and Joseph awoke.

"Mary?"

I can't! she cried again.

Get up, Mary and hang onto Elizabeth, said Gabriel.

I can't!

Get up. Hang on.

Suddenly Mary was on her knees, her hands clutching the mane of the little donkey, who braced herself calmly against Mary's weight. Suddenly she remembered the birth of her cousin Elizabeth's baby, and of all the other babies she'd seen enter this world. Suddenly she knew she could do it. Suddenly she felt like pushing hard and she pushed, hard, again and again, each push forcing a deep groan from her lips. In between pushes she closed her eyes. Never had she pushed so hard, pushed and been pushed from within.

"I'll get Miriam," Joseph said, struggling to his feet and heading for the ladder.

"No-oo," Mary wailed, and then a savage sound came from her throat, a command: "No! You stay! "

Joseph's eyes were round with fear.

"My back! Help me do this! Hold my back! Hold it! Help me!"

The glimmer that was Gabriel came closer. He whispered something in Joseph's ear. Joseph gave no sign of hearing him, but he turned back to Mary and knelt behind her, his hands bracing against her thin back. James and Mattias cowered in the corner, watching in frightened silence.

Miriam and her husband were stirring up above, wakened by the noise. Heavy footsteps sounded across the ceiling from the kitchen, and Miriam's face appeared in the open trapdoor at the top of the ladder. Gabriel glimmered over to where she was and whispered in her ear. Miriam became as one frozen, silent, and motionless.

Now it didn't feel like pain. It felt like work. Good work. *Great* work. Mary pushed with every ounce of her strength, and pushed again. And again. "You're such a strong girl," Joseph said, smoothing her hair from her eyes. "Good. Good, Mary. Good!"

"Good!" Mary shouted. "Good!" She gave another mighty push and then a great sigh, flopping forward on Elizabeth's soft flank and reaching under the blanket. "Give me," she whispered to Joseph, and he reached under the blanket, too, and brought out something tiny and purple. "His face," she said, her voice hoarse from shouting, and Joseph took the corner of his robe and wiped the baby's face clean. There was a tiny cry, and another. "In my bag," Mary whispered, and Joseph rummaged for the clean cloths she had brought with her from home.

Joseph tied one cloth in a hard knot at the top of the baby's cord and cut the rest off with his sharp knife. "Now wrap him up hard," she said, and they wound the baby in more clean cloths, until he looked like a little mummy, with just his head visible. He had a head of black hair. Then Mary leaned against Elizabeth and untied the strings of her blouse.

"How do babies know what to do?" she wondered dreamily, as she watched her baby find his dinner. For that matter, how had *she* known what to do? She looked around for Gabriel, but he was nowhere to be found.

She was so tired.

Orphans and Angels

IT WAS ALWAYS COLD in the hills once the sun went down, no matter how warm the day had been. The sheep huddled together for warmth, quiet for the most part, although once in a while one of them gave a sudden loud bawl, and then the others snuffled a bit and fell silent again. Maybe they have nightmares, Obadiah thought, and reflexively counted them once more. All present. Nobody was going anywhere tonight.

His brother Omer was playing his flute, as he did every night after all the sheep were in and supper was finished. Omer was the best flute player ever, anywhere. The king himself didn't have a better flute player than Omer. Out here the sound of his flute was clear and sweet on the cold night air. Usually Obadiah fell asleep to the sound, and didn't awaken until sunrise.

Obadiah had tended sheep with his brother for as long as he could remember. Omer remembered their parents, but Obadiah had been too little when they died. Sometimes he thought he remembered a soft lap, strong arms around him: his mother. But maybe not. The music of the flute always made him wonder about her. "Did she sing?" he would ask Omer. "What was her voice like?" And Omer would tell what he remembered, about their mother and their father, about their home, about the little stick horse that Obadiah used to ride around the house. Everything he remembered. "What happened to my horse?" Obadiah asked once. "I don't know," Omer said. "Burned, I guess."

Their house, burned. Their stable and their animals. Everything they owned. Only Omer and Obadiah had survived: their father had run back into the house and gotten them, thrown them both right out the window into the street below. He had thought their mother was out there waiting for them. But instead she had run screaming down into the stable to look for her little boys. The house collapsed in flames around them.

But a boy could live if he could walk; he could be a shepherd. Omer watched his uncle's sheep, and little Obadiah toddled along behind. Every day in summer they went out with the sheep, opening the door of the sheepfold and watching the animals stream out and head for the high meadows, where the grass was plentiful. In the winter, they stayed in the fold all day every day with the sheep, coming into town now and then for feed and supplies. Their home was not a house, with a mother and a father and a stick horse. But they had a roof over their heads, and they could eat.

Not much happened out there with the sheep: the life of one sheep is very much like the life of another. Obadiah knew the countryside, knew where the streams were, and the best meadows for grazing. He knew the plants. He certainly knew sheep. He knew lions and foxes and wolves, and how to protect against them: both he and Omer carried slingshots, and one of Obadiah's jobs was finding the right kinds of sharp stones to use in their slingshots. He wore a leather pouch around his skinny waist everywhere he went, and when he saw a good stone he would pick it up and put it in his pouch.

Today had been a good day for stones. Obadiah had found at least a dozen perfect ones, good, heavy, small stones with several sharp points. His pouch was weighed down with them by the end of the day—a good supply—and he had stopped looking when a flash of brilliant blue on the dusty path caught his eye. What was that? He had stooped to pick it up.

It was a gold ring with an enormous blue stone. The gem was held in place by the open beak of a golden bird, whose body formed the ring and whose talons grasped the other edge of the stone. It was heavy, and it was big: the ring filled the palm of Obadiah's hand.

He had looked around. He was alone on the path in the bright sun; only the sound of birds and the buzz of insects broke the stillness. Omer was up in the meadow. Nobody but Obadiah had seen the ring. Nobody else knew.

In all his life, Obadiah had never kept a secret from his brother. But now, he had put the ring into his leather pouch and headed up to the meadow. He had said nothing about it when he saw his brother. He just helped round all the sheep up, counted them several times as he always did, and walked, as always, at the back of the flock while Omer walked at the front until they reached the fold. During supper he was quiet, only responding when Omer spoke to him. He wasn't quite sure why he didn't want to tell his brother about the ring—they shared everything. But he knew he wouldn't tell him. He wouldn't tell anybody.

"You must be tired tonight," Omer told him. "You've hardly said a word."

"Yeah, I guess I am," Obadiah said. They were leaning against the gate, as they did every night. They always slept at the entrance to the fold in the summer. Omer played the flute and on clear nights like tonight they gazed at the stars, stars so fat and bright they seemed to lean out of the sky toward the earth, so that Obadiah felt he could reach out and pluck one down. One of them had been especially large lately; it was near the horizon now, hovering right over the city.

The flute sang to the darkness, its notes clear and sweet. Higher and higher they went, until Obadiah was sure the pure tones must be climbing to heaven itself. He gazed at the bright star and let the music carry him into sleep.

But the star seemed to follow him there, to appear in his dream, to fill it, so that its golden light was everywhere. And the music of the flute began to sound like words, not just notes.

Child!

Obadiah opened his eyes. A golden shimmer sat on the fence post. It was a shape, a shape of *something*, not a person but not a sheep, either. And it certainly wasn't his brother—Omer sat like a statue, his eyes staring straight ahead, his flute to his lips. But no sound came from the flute. Instead, the shimmer was speaking.

Child! it said again. Its voice was very *like* a flute. Obadiah looked at his motionless brother and back at the shimmer. It wasn't Omer. Obadiah felt the hairs on the back of his neck stand straight up. He could barely speak.

Who are you?

I'm Gabriel. The shimmer slipped from the post to the top rail of the gate, and Obadiah slid away and pressed himself hard against the opposite post, wishing with all his heart that they'd slept inside that night.

I don't know anyone named Gabriel. What do you want?

Just to talk to you.

It was the ring, Obadiah was certain. He should have left it right where it was, on the path. What had he been thinking? Now he was a jewel thief.

I can explain. I didn't mean to steal the ring. I just didn't know what it was. Whose it was, I mean. You can have it back. It's in my bag.

The ring? The shimmer shook all over, and there was a tinkling sound. Obadiah realized that it was laughing. *Oh, never mind about the ring. The ring will take care of itself.*

No, I'll get it, Obadiah said, desperately. Why wasn't Omer doing something about this? *Really. I don't want it. It's not mine. You can have it back and then you can go, all right?*

Well, not yet. You haven't heard what I have to tell you yet, Obadiah.

How do you know my name?

I know your parents.

My parents are dead.

Yes. Here, they are. But I'm not from here.

Where are you from? Obadiah asked, but he wasn't sure he really wanted to know. Surely it was time to wake up now. He squeezed his eyes tightly shut and gave himself a shake. Then he opened them. The sky was still dark, and the shimmer was still there.

Well, heaven. You know . . . up there. And all around. You know . . . heaven. With that, the shimmer shot straight up into the sky with a great whooshing sound, like the sound of the wind in a storm, faster than an arrow, faster than lightning. It hung there among the stars for a moment, indistinguishable from the rest of them. Then it exploded the whole sky in a burst of color and light that made the countryside as bright as high noon, the intense light stabbing Obadiah's eyes. Then the shimmer shot back down and settled again on the fencepost. Obadiah still could hardly see. His heart was pounding.

You know . . . up there.

I think I'd better go now.

Right you are. And before you go, I have a message just for you.

Um, I don't think it's for me.

It's for you all right. You're the one who found the ring, right?

Really, I don't want the ring. You can have it. Here, let me just . . . Obadiah started for his bag to retrieve the ring, but the shimmer was suddenly right next to him and he found that his legs wouldn't move. Neither would his arms. He couldn't even blink.

Something has happened in town. You need to go down there as soon as you can, and your brother, too.

We can't leave the sheep up here by themselves.

I'll take care of that. You have to get down there as soon as you can.

Omer won't leave them either. We can't.

The shimmer sighed, a sound like the tinkling of ice. Mary had been so easy to talk to, Gabriel said to himself. This boy simply had no sense of adventure.

I think you've seen what I can do. I think you'll agree that I can handle twenty sheep for a couple of hours. Suit yourself, Obadiah, but believe me when I tell you that your lives will change completely if you do as I tell you and that nothing will change if you don't. What you want most in all the world is down there. You have to go if you want it. Omer?

Gabriel turned toward Obadiah's motionless brother, who immediately stood up and tucked his flute into his belt. "Well, come on," he said. "You heard him. We've got to go."

Obadiah didn't understand. Omer had heard everything that was said, even though he had sat there the whole time like a statue? Omer was willing to leave the sheep in the care of someone they didn't know, someone who looked like a collection of stars? And another thing—Omer had heard the conversation about the ring!

"Oh, no!" Obadiah groaned out loud. But Omer was already on the path that led away from the sheepfold and toward the town, and Obadiah scrambled after him. He looked back. The sheep were silent and still. Obadiah saw that the shimmer was still atop the fence post, and that a shining ring of spangles encircled the sheepfold. Gabriel had paralyzed them, just as he had paralyzed Omer. Those sheep weren't going anywhere.

This world was not our home. We were visitors here.

Travelers

IF AHMED HAD KNOWN how long a journey this was going to be, he would have had the girth strap on the lead camel's enormous saddle replaced before they left. In fact, he would have had new girth straps put on all three kings' saddles, and on his own, too, if he'd known they were going to be on the road for more than *six months*. There would be a harness maker in Bethlehem, surely. Ahmed sighed as he tugged at the worn band of leather that encircled the camel, tightening it as hard as he dared for the night's travel.

There was nothing in the least unusual about their setting out on a rigorous journey of unknown length to an unknown destination. This sort of thing had been happening for as long as Ahmed had been in King Caspar's service. People from all over the world came to the palace to ask the wise old king questions about life and its meaning, and presumably they all departed more enlightened than they had been when they arrived. But Ahmed was used to getting vague answers, or none at all, when he asked his royal master for concrete information: "When do you wish to go to your summer palace by the sea? What would you like the cook to prepare for your supper? When will your judgment concerning the indigo merchants' quarrel with the weavers' guild be rendered?" Ahmed could not help but wonder about just how useful a thing wisdom was, sometimes: how was it that a person could be consulted by people all over the world about the meaning of life but couldn't remember how many children he had or find his way around his own home?

Even for King Caspar, though, this journey was a strange one: on this journey, they traveled only at night. This was because they were following a star, and everybody knows that stars only come out at night. When Ahmed asked his master why they should follow a star rather than consulting a map, the response was an absent-minded smile and an incomprehensible mumble. It had been hard on the camels, who had grown to adulthood sleeping at night and traveling during the day, like everybody else; they didn't take kindly their new nocturnal life. It was even harder on Ahmed, to whose lot it fell to get them going every evening, at just about the time when a normal camel likes to call it a day.

And now there were three kings to manage, not just one. Ahmed found it hard to believe, but it was true: his master was not the only monarch in the world whose subjects didn't seem to mind if he sat and thought all day instead of attending to whatever it is that kings do. There were two others traveling with them, each as vague as King Caspar, if not more so. So it was three camels, three saddles, three trunks of fine clothing to keep track of. And the presents.

This trip seemed to be about the presents. An ebony casket filled with gold, a silver box filled with fragrant incense and a large alabaster flask containing oil of myrrh rode behind Ahmed in his saddlebag. The idea was that there was a fourth king being born wherever it was they were headed, and that these three would visit him and bring him presents and then they would head home. That was it.

The journey was hard. Ahmed's whole body was sore at the end of every night's journey, and he was decades younger than the youngest of the three kings. They should have been in agony, but they showed no signs of discomfort: they smiled their serene, vague smiles at him when he approached them with a question or a warning, thanked him gently when he brought them food. They spoke little to one another, content instead to keep their gaze on the heavens and think their own inscrutable thoughts.

The main thing, though, was to get them through whatever task they had set themselves and get them home again in one piece, and it looked to Ahmed as if they were close to halfway there. And so, while he was far too serious a man ever to let his guard down fully, he reconsidered his annoyance at the vagueness of the whole project and began to hum to himself as he finished preparing for the night's travel. The star was right above the horizon; for certain, it marked a spot in Bethlehem, the very next little town they would reach.

Reaching it would require a curious retracing of their steps—they had passed through these hills once already, only a couple of days ago. The kings had thought it proper to pay a visit to their Judean counterpart, who had received them warmly. Now *that* was a proper king, as far as Ahmed was concerned: King Herod was wiry and energetic, shouting orders at his servants, signing documents with his signet ring as they talked, barking clipped questions at his mild visitors while they sat and drank their tea. King Herod's reception area was elegant, luxurious, and *orderly*—Ahmed appreciated this, as he was always embarrassed when dignitaries came to call on King Caspar, whose every table overflowed with books and scrolls, whose astrolabes and sextants sat jumbled together on every available surface, so that there was hardly room for a visitor to set down so much as a pair of gloves, if he ever wanted to see them again. The reception area of Ahmed's royal master looked more like a secondhand merchant's stall at the local bazaar than like a king's chambers.

As quiet as the kings had been on the journey, they seemed to come alive in King Herod's presence, and conversation about the birth of the new king went on into the night. Court astrologers and sages were summoned and dismissed;

the peculiarly dressed priests and scribes of the Jewish people were sent for, arriving only half awake but already expounding on their sacred writings, even as they rubbed the sleep from their eyes. Years of service at court had taught Ahmed the art of hearing every word of a conversation while appearing not to listen to it at all, and he listened intently to this one.

These monarchs were not interested in the fact that the new king was to be king of the *Jews*—none of Ahmed's masters were Jews and all of them were kings. But they knew the writings of which the Jewish sages spoke, had read them in the odd Greek into which they had been translated by Jews who lived outside of what they considered their Holy Land, this insular little country to which they now traveled. This tiny country and its people were the key to something that was transforming the entire world, they believed, and not just the world: the heavens themselves were on the move.

It was this tremendous news they wanted to share with Herod. Very soon, they told Herod, none of them would be kings! Everything was changing. Very soon, they said, the world itself would look nothing like it looked now. What it would be like occupied their discussion, and opinions varied, but one thing was certain: change was coming, and it was coming now. Maybe it was already here.

The old kings were excited about laying down their crowns. They'd been kings all their lives and hadn't set much store by any of it, much preferring their studies to their royal powers. They talked about the end of the world as they knew it with the giddiness of children about to be taken to the circus. There seemed to be nothing fearsome about it, in their minds: this world was a shadow, they told each other, over and over again. This world was not our home. We were visitors here, unwilling ones at that, strangers. And now we were about to be restored to our proper place.

Ahmed could tell that Herod viewed it differently. He wasn't interested in change, at least not in any change that wasn't his idea. He had no intention of laying down his crown any time soon. Ahmed watched Herod weigh the chatter of the old kings. He listened as his own seers corroborated their testimony, his thin lips becoming a grim line as they cited ancient texts, the positions of stars, the possible meaning of the new star they claimed to have discovered in the western sky. Herod's face grew darker with every word, as the sages continued to talk, but of course the old men didn't notice. Ahmed did, though, and began to feel a little uneasy. Ever since coming to serve King Caspar, he had been impatient with his master's otherworldliness. Now, for the first time in his life, he found himself preferring it to the ruthlessness he was beginning to perceive in the face and demeanor of the younger king.

The conversation went much too late, in Ahmed's opinion, for the health of his elderly master. There was no point at all in trying to catch King Caspar's eye; subtle signals were lost on him in the best of circumstances, and the old king was much too absorbed in the conversation to notice any now. Finally, though, the evening came to an end, and the kings were ushered off to sleeping quarters in the royal residence.

They would leave in the late afternoon, after King Herod's own harness maker had installed fine new girth straps on all the camels' saddles. The town was just five miles from the palace. So tomorrow was the night when the new king would receive his unusual gifts.

THIS IS WHAT IT IS

TO BE HAPPY

Visitors

Obadiah and Omer walked quickly and surely down toward the town in the dark; the path was treacherous enough even in the daytime, but they were familiar with every inch of the hills. From a distance, it looked as if the lights of Bethlehem were all lit: it seemed that everyone was still awake, as late as it was. And once in awhile, another light: a shimmer here and there just ahead of them: *You are on the right track. Keep walking this way.* And, once they had passed through the city gates, the shimmer appeared again, lighting the gutters and the doorways as it passed.

The boys' progress through the crowded streets was swift. What was it that waited here for them, Obadiah wondered as they hurried along? What was the thing that would bring Obadiah what he wanted most in all the world? What did he really want, anyway, that he did not have? His life was not a bad one, really. It was true that he had no parents, but he had no real memory of ever having had any, so he did not feel this as the loss he knew it was. He and Omer had each other. It was true that he stood little chance of ever being anything but a shepherd, but that was all right, really—Obadiah liked sheep.

And yet the shimmering Gabriel had come to him, not to Omer, who *did* have longings, who *could* be something more than a shepherd, who *did* have memories of home that made him sad. And Gabriel had been insistent: *Your lives will change completely if you do what I tell you. And nothing will change if you don't.*

Well, all right, Obadiah thought. Maybe Gabriel came to me for Omer's sake. That made some sense. Obadiah would have done anything for his brother.

That was, in fact, the whole reason he had kept the ring a secret. Surely that ring must be worth money—a lot of money, more money than either boy had ever seen, which was hardly any money at all. Someday it would be possible to send Omer somewhere, somewhere where his flute would make him famous. Somewhere *else*. Obadiah hadn't a clue where that might be, but he knew for sure it wasn't the Judean hill country. Maybe shimmering Gabriel was right; maybe something wonderful was about to happen. Obadiah remembered the blinding light, the shimmer shooting like lightning into the sky, the terrifying soundless explosion in the heavens, and he decided that Gabriel was probably right about most things.

They turned down an alleyway that came to an end at the back entrance to an inn. It was the stable entrance. The shimmer lingered for a moment, outlining the door, then dissipated into a soft glow that filled the stable. A boy sat leaning against the doorpost.

"Lady just had a baby in there," said the boy.

"Is everything all right?" asked Omer. He and Obadiah had helped birth scores of lambs in their short lives. Although they'd never attended a human birth, Omer didn't reckon it could be all that different.

"Guess so. Nothin' wrong with his lungs, anyway." As if to demonstrate the truth of this statement, a lusty howl went up from inside the stable, followed by the soft murmur of a woman's voice and a man's quiet chuckle. Another boy came to the door and stared at the two young visitors.

"Hello," he said. "I'm James."

"Oh, yeah," said the first boy. "I'm Mattias. Who are you?"

"I'm Omer, and this is my brother Obadiah. We keep our uncle's sheep about a mile from here."

"Can we see the baby?" Obadiah asked James.

"I guess so," James answered. "Come on in. Watch your head."

Omer couldn't straighten to his full height under the low ceiling of the stable. The shimmer of the angel who had led them through town lit the room enough so that they could see its occupants: a sleeping donkey, a cow chewing her cud and staring at nothing, a man, a woman, and a swaddled baby. A canvas sling filled with provisions hung from the rafters, safe from marauding mice, and a few parcels wrapped in blankets sat in the corner on top of a leather saddle.

The woman was really just a girl—Omer's age, or maybe even a little younger. Bits of straw clung to her hair, and there was a smudge of blood on one of her cheeks. But her face was radiant as she gazed at her baby, who lay in the crook of her arm as she reclined on a blanket. An older woman was gathering up the soiled sheets for washing, chattering with great animation to no one in particular about her own horrifying experience of childbirth, which could not have been recent.

The man looked up sharply as the boys entered, his hand at his belt and his face watchful. "Who are you?"

The old woman stopped what she was doing and came closer to Omer. "Well, I know you! My Lord, Omer, look at you! I remember you when you were just a little boy and now look at the size of you."

Omer was embarrassed. "Um, hello, ma'am."

"Well, you were just a little boy when you lived here. Oh, Lord, I remember the night your house burned down like it was yesterday. You two little boys."

The woman looked up at Omer in the dim light, her bundle of cloth still on her hip. Obadiah felt something move in his chest, something like a click. He had lived near this house when he was little. This lady remembered his mother. It seemed suddenly that his mother was nearby, that he might reach out and touch her.

The baby gave a cry, and Mary began to rock him gently back and forth. Obadiah took a step forward and knelt down in the straw to look at the little face. "Can I hold him?" He surprised himself at his own boldness.

Mary motioned for him to sit and settled the little bundle carefully in his lap. Obadiah hadn't held a baby person before; only baby sheep. "What happened to your mother?" Mary asked him.

"We had a fire," Obadiah said. He'd never told anyone about this before; he'd never had to—he'd never talked to anybody who didn't already know about it. "My mother tried to save Omer and me. And my father tried to save her. And so they both burned."

"They were brave, your parents," Mary said. "They loved you more than they loved their own life."

"Yes," Obadiah said. "I don't remember them. My brother does, though."

"I'll bet you wish you did."

"Yes." It was odd—Omer really didn't think about his parents much. But tonight he wished with all his heart that he had known them, wished that they were still alive. Wished it with a pang of loneliness that, he realized with a shock, was very familiar. He realized that he had always missed his mother and father. He had just never known it.

"So what are you doing out so late?"

Obadiah paused. Should he tell a stranger his story? He decided that he should. He told her about everything that had happened on this most peculiar day—about shimmering Gabriel and the way he could paralyze people and how he'd paralyzed the sheep so he and Omer could leave them and come down here, because Gabriel said that their lives would change completely if he came. It all sounded impossible, he knew. But Mary just listened and nodded. Of all the people in Bethlehem to whom Obadiah might have told his tale, Mary was surely the best one to understand it—nothing Gabriel might say or do would surprise her. The only part of the story that Obadiah left out was the beautiful, blue-stoned ring.

"And what is it in your life that's going to change completely?" Mary asked when he was finished.

"I don't know," Obadiah said. "I can't think of anything, really—I just watch my sheep, and I don't mind. But my brother, he needs to be somewhere else."

"Where does he need to be?" Mary asked.

"My brother is the best flute player in the world. He's better than anyone else here, even people who have played for years and years—they say so themselves. He shouldn't be a shepherd. He should be a king's musician."

"Really? I'd love to hear him." She turned to Omer. "Did you bring your flute with you? Could you play us a lullaby?"

"Mary sings," Joseph told Omer. "Like a bird."

"Oh, not really," Mary said with a smile.

"Yes, really," said Joseph. He moistened the corner of a rag with water and leaned toward her. "We missed a spot," he said, and wiped the little smudge from her cheek.

Obadiah watched this simple display of tenderness with that same strange feeling in his chest, like a click, as Omer took his flute out of his bag and began to play a lullaby everybody knew. The notes were pure and sweet. He dipped his head and his flute at Mary, and she began to sing along: "The sparrow has found her a house, and the swallow a nest where she may lay her young . . ." Into the dark night they sang, Mary and the flute, song after song, and Obadiah listened. This was what it was to be happy—he understood. Your chest can get so full of happiness that it almost hurts.

The old lady appeared at the top of the ladder leading to the house. "Mattias, climb up here and get this tray, will you?" The boy clambered up the ladder and crept carefully back down with the tray, piled with raisin cakes. Then she handed him down a steaming jug of tea. "Mary, you must be hungry. Me, I could eat have eaten a horse after each one of mine. And you boys, outside all night. You must be starving, too."

The music stopped abruptly. The tea was sweet with honey, and the raisins plump and delicious. The innkeeper's wife seemed to have a limitless supply of the lovely little cakes, and several trays of them were consumed.

Mary and Joseph leaned against Elizabeth the donkey, dozing off now and then while Omer resumed playing the flute softly and the younger boys took turns fussing over the baby, who slept through it all, waking only a few times to nurse. Mary let them watch as she changed his diaper, and the baby caught Mattias right in the face with a remarkably well-aimed stream of pee, provoking gales of laughter from Obadiah and James.

"I wouldn't laugh, James," Joseph told his son, with a smile. "Your time will come."

An Intruder

It was probably early morning now. The city outside had become quiet at last, and it was still pitch-dark, but a few birds were beginning to stir. Obadiah, Mattias, and James were all curled up under the same blanket at the bottom of the ladder, and Mary and Joseph lay on another blanket with the baby between them. Omer, his flute beside him, was sound asleep, wrapped in his cloak and leaning against the door of the stable. Soon the brothers would head back up into the hills, where their sheep waited to be taken up to a fresh meadow for another day's grazing.

Suddenly Omer started awake. There was a noise outside: soft footsteps, like someone trying not to be heard. The noise stopped. Someone was right outside the door.

Silently, Omer took his sling and a sharp stone from his bag. In an instant, he was loaded and ready. He sat motionless, listening. The intruder pushed against the door quietly, but it was thick and heavy. Both he and Omer waited. On his second push, Omer was ready, and he flung the door open, spilling the man onto the dirt floor of the stable.

Ahmed gave a yelp and lay stunned for a moment. A ragged boy stood over him with a loaded sling poised an arm's length from Ahmed's right eye. Joseph sprang forward and grabbed both of Ahmed's wrists in his own powerful hands, pinning his arms behind his back. Mary, too frightened to scream, held the baby close to her breast.

Ahmed thought fast. "Where is he that is born King of the Jews?" he whispered.

A piece
of
her
mother's
wisdom.

Things Come Together

As SOON AS HE HEARD this question, Joseph relaxed his painful grip on Ahmed's wrists and began to laugh. "It's another adventure, Mary."

Mary was giggling by now, too. "Well, we're overdue for one. We haven't had an adventure in at least four hours. I was getting bored."

Obadiah looked at the man sitting on the floor rubbing his wrists. His clothes and turban were simple but rich, and his beard was trimmed to an elegant point, not bushy and unruly like Joseph's beard. He was no Israelite. "He's right here," he told the stranger. "That baby right there's the King of the Jews."

He pointed to the baby, who began to whimper. Before Ahmed could respond, King Caspar appeared at the door and made his way inside. He looked at the little bundle and smiled his vague smile. "Well, now, aren't you a fine king?" he said, as much to himself as to anyone else. "Hello, there, young man." He waggled a gloved finger at the baby, who was now in full howl.

King Caspar's robe for this occasion was of silver thread on brilliant blue wool, and his turban was enormous, a complicated edifice of brilliant white silk. To his horror, Obadiah saw that it was pinned in front with an enormous blue stone clutched in the talons of a golden bird, a jewel identical in every respect to the ring he had found. There could be no doubt that this old king was the ring's rightful owner.

The two other kings crowded in. Having paid so little attention for so many years to the luxury of their own homes, they barely noticed that they were in a stable filled with animals and urchins; their eyes were on the child. They nudged one another excitedly and chattered in a language no one else in the room understood. Ahmed the servant man hurried back and forth, bringing in trunks and bags, unrolling carpets for the kings to sit on, settling each king on a large cushion. At last all was arranged, and each king held his gift in his lap.

The presentation of the gifts took a while. Each one was accompanied by an earnest and lengthy explanation of its significance, which Ahmed translated as best he could. Joseph answered each king to the best of his ability, hoping that the translator upon whose accuracy he depended didn't hold a grudge. More raisin cakes and more tea were handed down from upstairs, and this time the innkeeper and his wife came down the ladder to meet the three kings—until now, no royalty had honored their little inn with a visit.

The unusual gifts were offered and accepted, compliments were paid to the innkeeper's wife for her delicious raisin cakes, the baby's long eyelashes were extravagantly admired, the happy kings exclaimed over the child they thought would change the world. And all the while, Obadiah sat in silent misery. In his imagination, the heavy ring in his leather bag grew more enormous by the minute, as he agonized over when and how to return it to its rightful owner.

"What's the trouble?" Mary whispered. She had tucked the baby into his makeshift cradle for a nap while the adults talked, and made her way over to the corner where Obadiah was sitting. "You're so quiet. Don't you feel well?"

The tears Obadiah had been fighting ever since he saw the jewel on King

Caspar's turban spilled from his eyes and ran down his cheeks, and he turned toward the wall so the other boys wouldn't see him cry. He told Mary everything: about finding the ring, about not telling anyone, about thinking the ring might buy Omer the chance to become a court musician, even though Obadiah didn't really know how a person became a court musician, about probably being hung for being a jewel thief.

"Well, you're not a thief at all," Mary began. "You didn't steal the ring. You just found it on the path."

"They'll never believe me."

"Of course they will. Look at them. I think they'd believe just about anything." They looked over at the three kings. They were asking Ahmed to tell the innkeeper that, in their opinion, the straw on his stable floor was not straw at all any more, but was now really gold in the *form* of straw, and they were arranging to buy it all from him in exchange for a medium-sized trunk full of golden coins. The innkeeper, astounded at his good fortune, kept asking Ahmed to repeat himself. His wife sat on the bottom step of the ladder, her tray of raisin cakes at her feet and her face buried in her capacious apron, weeping for joy.

Maybe Mary was right. The kings seemed to have the best of intentions. But even though Obadiah couldn't keep the ring, not now that he knew whose it was—that really *would* be stealing—he just couldn't figure out when to tell him.

"Well, how about right now?" Mary asked, as if she had read his mind, and she stood up, reaching for his hand. She led him to where the kings sat in a row.

"And who are you, young man?" King Caspar asked kindly.

"I'm Obadiah and this is my brother, Omer." Obadiah looked around for Omer, who came forward with a concerned look on his face. What was his brother doing, addressing a king directly without being addressed first?

"And what do you do?"

"We're sheepherders, sir," said Omer. "We're on our way back up to the meadow now."

"They're shepherds," the old king said triumphantly, looking at the king on his right hand. "What do you know about that?"

"Shepherds!" the other king said, and beamed approvingly on the two boys, as if he had just been told they'd happened upon a method for turning baser metals into gold. "I suppose you herd sheep, then?"

"Um, yes, sir, we do. We herd sheep. And we're going to go and herd sheep right now," Omer said, grabbing one of Obadiah's arms firmly and turning him toward the door. "It was an honor to meet you, sir. All you sirs." Omer gave an awkward bow intended to encompass all three kings at once. He placed one hand on Obadiah's head and pushed it in the direction of the floor, causing his brother to perform something rather like a bow.

"Wait. I have to give you something." Obadiah fished in his stone bag and drew forth the ring. "I found this on the path and I think it's yours." He held out the ring to King Caspar.

"Oh, ho, look at that! You found it! See that! He found the ring! Ha! Oh, yes. Very good! Young man, young Obadiah, is it? What did I tell you? I left it just for you to find, young man! Oh, glorious!"

Ahmed sighed and closed his eyes, praying inwardly for patience. He had turned their baggage inside out seven times, looking for the ring, but his master had deliberately left it on the path, as if it were nothing more than a bread crumb. The kings were all smiles, pointing at Obadiah and nodding their heads. "Oh, God is so good!"

"He is?" Obadiah had never thought much about whether God was good or not. God was just God. He resolved to give the matter more thought from now on.

"Oh, he is," said Mary, turning back toward the place where the baby slept, like a little angel. Well, maybe not very much like an angel, given what Mary now knew about angels.

"It's yours," Obadiah said again, holding out the ring to King Caspar.

"No, boy, it's all yours," the old king laughed. "What do I need with a ring? This shadow world is coming to an end." The other kings nodded happily. "We need to get back to Herod right away and let him know we've found the new king!"

Mary's heart skipped a beat. King Herod? She looked at Joseph, whose eyes narrowed in sudden suspicion.

"No," she began, but a sudden shimmer enveloped the three kings and transfixed them in mid-conversation, King Caspar's finger upraised to make a point. It only lasted a moment, but when it was over, it seemed to have erased the idea of a return visit to King Herod from their minds.

"Well, Ahmed, we'd best be going. Maybe we'll go and see what it's like to be a sheepherder, shall we, lads? You know, one of the kings of this country was a shepherd in his youth, I believe, and . . ." King Caspar subsided into a long discussion of the Hebrew psalms, as the other two kings listened with great interest and Ahmed scurried back and forth with his boxes, carpets, and bundles of straw. James, Omer, and Obadiah took pity on him, and helped him saddle and load the camels.

At last the kings were mounted and ready to leave. Mary, Joseph, and James stood outside the stable door to say good-bye, the baby wide-eyed and solemn in Mary's arms. Omer and Obadiah would lead the way up to the hill country on foot, with Ahmed on his camel bringing up the rear.

"Queen of Heaven," King Caspar said to Mary, bowing to her from high on his camel. "We will meet again. The world is coming to an end."

"Ah. Well, have a lovely trip," Mary answered. She had learned that a person didn't necessarily have to respond with great precision when King Caspar talked like that. She'd leave the end of the world to take care of itself. Queen of Heaven, indeed!

Just then the boy Mattias ran up, out of breath. His face was a mask of shock and horror.

"Soldiers!" he gasped, "They're in the town! They're killing babies!"

There was no time to lose. The innkeeper and his wife were dispatched to the front of the house to sit watch on the bench there and look like what they were: people whose childrearing years were long past. Joseph grabbed the canvas bag and stuffed the kings' gifts into it, covering them with blankets and their one cooking pot, filled with more raisin cakes from their hostess. Obadiah held the baby while Mary roused Elizabeth and led her quickly out the door. Ahmed took the canvas bag and placed it on Elizabeth's back as if it were a saddle, tying two enormous bags of the golden straw on top of it. He knelt Caspar's camel and lifted Mary into the saddle in front of the old king. Obadiah handed her the baby and the camel stood. Joseph grabbed his staff and became a shepherd, leading Elizabeth, packed with what looked like provisions. Within ten minutes they were gone.

The trip back up to the sheepfold took longer than the trip down. The way up was steep and rocky, but Omer didn't dare go by way of the road or even the shepherds' path—a wise decision, for they encountered no one as they climbed. It was still morning when they arrived at the fold. The sheep were still there, of course, still and silent, just as they had been left. In the bright sun, it was difficult to see the shimmer of their angel guardians, but it was easy to tell when they departed: all the sheep began to bleat at once, and to jostle one another toward the gate. Obadiah opened it and they streamed out into the meadow.

"We're safe here," Mary said. "They're in the town."

"This is all our doing," King Caspar said, his old voice quavering. "We should never have come. We should never have visited Herod. We led him here. We are responsible for the murder of all those children."

"With respect, sir, that is Herod's doing, not yours," said Joseph, "and he is responsible. No one but ourselves is responsible for the things we do."

King Caspar took Joseph's large hand in both of his gloved ones and peered up at him. "You will be a good father to the Son of God. You will teach him well."

Joseph was emboldened by the king's words. "Sir, we are out of immediate danger but not out of all danger. The innkeeper's wife is a generous soul. But she will talk, and people will find out about us. We won't be safe on the road back to our home. Even if we ourselves escape harm, we may leave behind the same path of death and destruction in every place we are seen."

"What do you propose?"

"I want you to take us with you back to your country." Joseph chose his words carefully. "James and I are carpenters and we can be useful to you. I can make anything. I will do anything I have to do to protect my family. I need to get them away from here."

"But of course we will take you! Oh, God is good! Who am I, an old man in this shadow world, to receive such an honor? Ahmed, it is a long journey. We will stop in the kingdoms of each of my friends here, and then we will reach our home. Our company will be . . . ah, enlarged. See to our guests."

Obadiah appeared at the king's elbow. "You need us to go with you. Omer and me."

"My boy?"

"You have no weapons and soldiers are after you. Omer and I can kill a lion at a hundred paces with our slingshots. That king you were talking about, King David—he killed a giant with his slingshot when he was no bigger than me."

"Is that a fact?"

"Yes. With one stone. Right between the eyes. Went down like a tree. And you also need music." Obadiah thought he might as well bring it up while he had the king's attention.

"Music?" The old king was confused.

"My brother is the best flute player in the world. The baby likes his music and it helps him sleep. You need a traveling court musician for the baby."

"Ahmed, do I need a traveling court musician?"

"I believe so, sir."

"Ah, well, then. Good! We'll all go, shall we?"

"We can't all go. What about the sheep?" asked Omer.

"Somebody will be up to check on you soon, because of the trouble," Ahmed said. "They'll find the sheep in the fold."

"Yes," said the king, "Oh, and leave them a box of gold, will you? To compensate them for the loss of these most excellent boys? After all, the world is coming to an end."

So the traveling plans were made: They would all rest now in the sheepfold and set out again at nightfall. They would continue by night until they left Judea, when it would be safer to move by day. Mary and the baby rested under the outcropping of rock at the back of the sheepfold, out of sight of anyone who might pass by. The adventure was not over, it seemed—an even longer journey lay ahead. Their family was larger now, and might just stay that way. Mary had a houseful of boys to take care of: real boys, not thirty-seven imaginary babies.

How was her mother? Would she ever see her again? Anna was at home, she knew, cooking in their kitchen, working in her garden, thinking about Mary, as Mary was thinking about her. Every loaf of bread she baked, every garden she planted, every little shirt she sewed for her son was a piece of her mother's wisdom. There would not be a day she wouldn't think of her, no matter how far from home she traveled. Joseph would find a way to get word to Mary's parents from wherever it was they were going.

Or maybe a shimmer would appear in Anna's kitchen one day, and no further explanation would be needed.

※